CHRISTMAS

COLORING BOOK FOR KIDS AGES 4-8

32 Coloring Book Pages For All Children, Girls and Boys

HO!
HO!
HO!
25

MerrY Christmas

Merry Christmas

DECEMBER
25

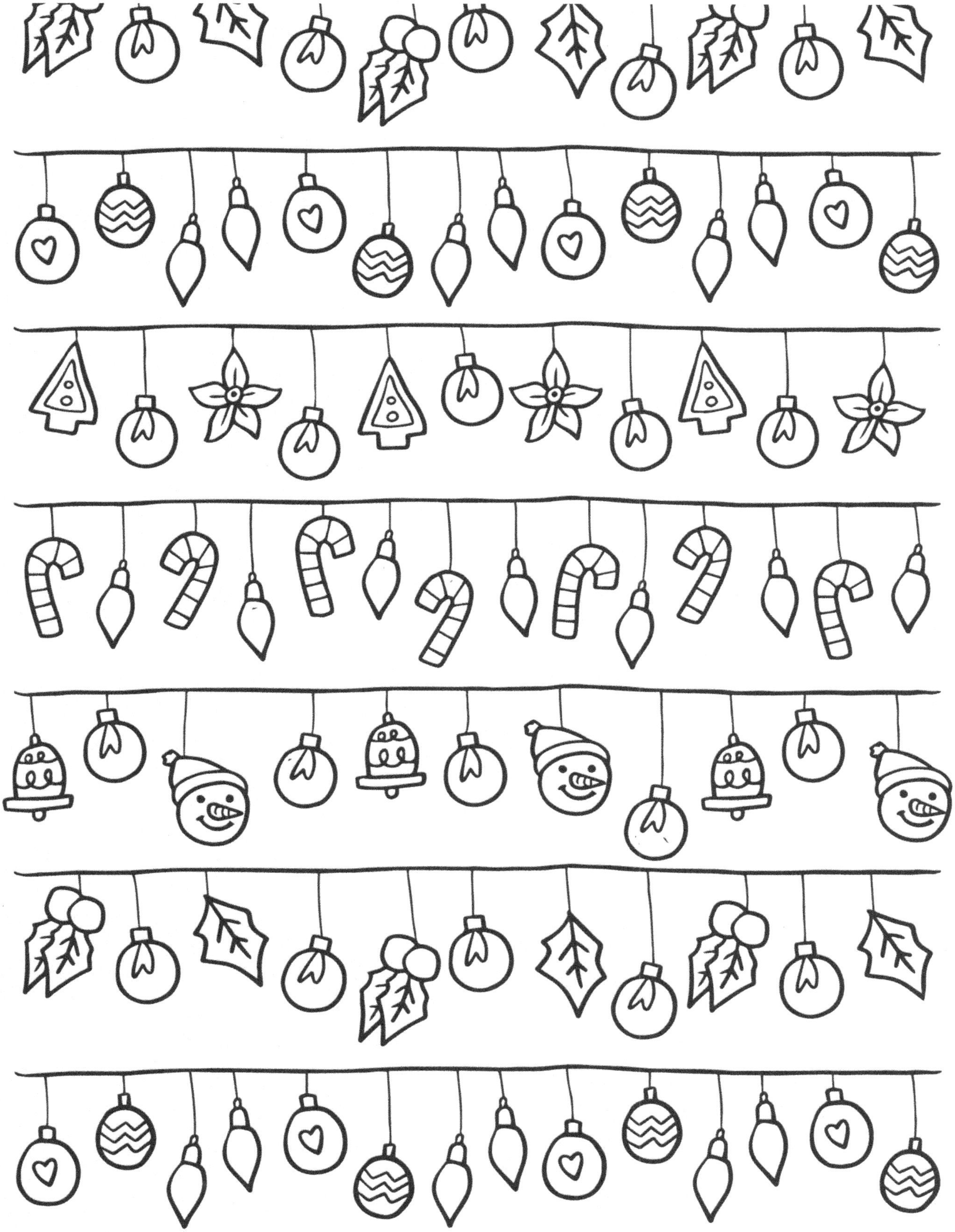

Merry
Christmas

Merry Christmas

15301376R00038

Made in the USA
Middletown, DE
21 November 2018